ANECDO

WENDY COPE

Anecdotal Evidence

~

FABER & FABER

First published in 2018
by Faber & Faber Ltd
Bloomsbury House
74–77 Great Russell Street
London WC1B 3DA

Typeset by Hamish Ironside
Printed in England by TJ International Ltd. Padstow

A CIP record for this book is available from the British Library

ISBN 978-0-571-33860-3 (hbk)
ISBN 978-0-571-33861-0 (pbk)

4 6 8 10 9 7 5 3

To Adèle and Sophie

Acknowledgements

Areté, Dark Horse, Eborakon, Eildon Tree, Festschrift for Fleur Adcock, Footnotes, The Guardian, Jubilee Lines (Faber), *Mail on Sunday, New Statesman, On Shakespeare's Sonnets* (Bloomsbury), *Poetry Ireland, Say Cheese* (Rockhurst Press), The Shakespeare Birthplace Trust website, *The Spectator, The Telegraph, Times Literary Supplement, 101 Poems to See You Through* (Ebury Press).

The Shakespeare poems (except for 'On Sonnet 22') were commissioned by The Shakespeare Birthplace Trust. They have been published by Celandine Press in a limited edition booklet. 'A Wreath for George Herbert' was commissioned by Shakespeare's Globe. 'Lantern Carol' was commissioned by the Ely Choral Society and has been set to music by Andrew Parnell. 'A Vow' has been set to music by Jools Holland.

Some of these poems were written during a month as poet in residence to the Stratford-on-Avon Poetry Festival. My thanks to Paul Edmondson of the Shakespeare Birthplace Trust for arranging the residency and to Sarah Hosking of the Hosking Houses Trust for providing accommodation in the Trust's cottage outside Stratford.

Contents

ANECDOTAL EVIDENCE

Evidence

'A great deal of anecdotal evidence suggests
that we respond positively to birdsong.'
– scientific researcher, *Daily Telegraph*, 8 February 2012

Centuries of English verse
Suggest the selfsame thing:
A negative response is rare
When birds are heard to sing.

What's the use of poetry?
You ask. Well, here's a start:
It's anecdotal evidence
About the human heart.

The Damage to the Piano

You can barely see
the damage to the piano
where the new bookcase knocked it,
but all hell would break loose
if my mother were here.

I sit for several minutes,
pondering the silence
where I am cast adrift
with all this furniture
and no-one to tell me off.

Baggage

Two smart porters carry luggage on
The label from the Nacional, Madrid.
The one from the hotel in Carcassonne
Features the fortress. That's stuck on the lid.
Some are partly missing. This one here
Says Vichy, and another Lac de Co . . .
Some scraps remain mysterious as to where
My father travelled all those years ago.
His sturdy leather suitcase, left too long
In our damp garage, still looks glamorous
To me. It calls to mind the handsome, young
And happy man I'd like to think he was.
The child of his old age, I close my eyes
And join him under sunny foreign skies.

Orb

An illuminated orb
against a black background –
the colour of flesh, with faint
red lines that could be rivers.

Not a planet in the night sky:
my eyeball
on the optician's screen.

It's beautiful. Just one small feature
of a mysterious universe
I'll never explore, packed neatly
in this soft container.

We know so little of ourselves,
and of each other – the working parts
we carry everywhere,

the darkness we scan
like astronomers, seeking
the half-forgotten stories of our lives.

1952

Sometimes, instead of a farthing,
shops give you safety pins.
Can that be right? I'm sure
it's what the teacher said.

I know it was 1952
because the same teacher, a nun,
announced one morning
that the King had died.

We were encouraged to go
to the chapel, to pray for his soul.
A Catholic friend showed me
what you do with the holy water.

It was lovely in there –
white, gold, pastels –
as pretty as the scenery
for the last act of a pantomime.

It may have been the same day
that I upset my mother
by asking for a rosary.
Soon after that,

as we sat down in a theatre,
where I couldn't make a fuss,
she told me it had been decided:
boarding school, next term.

Bags

After all these years
I've begun using it again –
the laundry bag embroidered
by Nanna: W. M. COPE LINEN
in large, neat red letters.

There's another bag somewhere,
a smaller one, with
W. M. COPE SHOES
embroidered in purple.
I've been trying to find it

to carry my shoes in
while snow is on the ground.
I have other fabric bags –
dozens of cotton ones
from libraries and festivals –

but I want the one Nanna made,
the one that hung in a cold
cloakroom until it was time
to pull on wellingtons
and trudge up the path to lessons.

I see that little girl
on an icy morning, with her shoe bag,
and I think of the grandmother
who couldn't prevent her
from being sent away

but spent hours making
things she could take with her
when she went to a place
where she didn't know anyone
and nobody knew her name.

Upheavals

When I was home in the holidays
I dreaded going back to school.
On the last day my mother and I
usually doubled our unhappiness
by having a row about the packing.

Once I had settled down at school,
I was fine. I didn't long for home
or for my parents until,
on a couple of Saturdays every term,
they came to take me out.

Sometimes we went to Lympne Airport
and watched cars being loaded
on to planes. The nose opened
and they went in from the front,
like something being swallowed by a whale –

a whale that could lift itself
and its heavy load into the air
for the short journey to France.
It was interesting enough to lift
my spirits a little. And there was tea.

But I remember those Saturdays
as heavy with the knowledge
that they would soon be over,
with the thought of parting
and homesickness and tears.

As I launched myself once more
into school life with friends
and teachers, the burden grew lighter.
I was all right. I wished
my parents would leave me alone.

Absent Friends

Roz

My school friend Roz, who died twenty years ago,
pulled her cardigan down at the back
every time she stood up and crossed a room.

Whenever I glance in a mirror
and see that my cardigan has ridden up
I remember Roz.

She was my rival in English.
The teachers were so impressed
by her passion for Tolkien
that I didn't read *The Lord of the Rings*
until I was fifty-five.

Julia

Julia, dear Julia,
taught me, one afternoon
in a shop in Chislehurst,
how to choose a card.
'That one is vulgar.
This one is too sweet.'

She's dead now
but her taste lives on.
I never buy a birthday or
a Christmas card
without asking myself
if she would approve.

2

She rang me in the holidays
and told me she was doing
a chapter of Caesar every day.
I followed her example
and passed the exam.

The last time I saw her
she was dying, bravely,
of motor neurone disease.
She couldn't speak. She wrote notes
that made us laugh.

That's an example
I may need to follow one day –
harder than translating Caesar,
but, if I think of Julia,
perhaps I'll pass the test.

Reunion

Fifty years have passed since we first met,
And forty-seven since we said goodbye,
Embarking on our adult lives – and yet
You are the same, it seems to me. Am I?
Five decades of life, of ups and downs,
Of love and marriage, work and motherhood,
And here we are, back in the world of gowns
And college food and essays – and it's good,
It's very good, my lovely, clever friends,
To travel to the past and find you here,
To share just one more evening meal that ends
In someone's room – before we disappear
Into a future, where I'm sad to know
It's over. It was over long ago.

An Afternoon

The two of them are sitting on the bed
In my small student room. My second year.
My parents are both feeling very sad
After a funeral not far from here:
My mother's closest girlhood friend, who died
Of cancer in her forties. They agree
They can't face driving home just yet, decide
To come and spend an hour or two with me.
And I, for once, am genuinely pleased
To see them. I'm depressed. I haven't said.
I hope the hugs and smiles I gave them eased
Their grief. Years later, when they're dead,
I will remember and be moved to say
I never loved them more than on that day.

1972

It was the year
of the hippy librarians from Islington.
My flatmate met hers first
and I got off with his friend.

They had beards. They smoked dope.
They were very alternative.
Mine gave me a copy
of *Vedanta for the Western World*.

I wore long Indian dresses
and tried to like the smell of joss sticks.
In August we sat in bed
and watched the Olympics, stoned.

Late that year I went into analysis.
Freud didn't get along
with the hippy boyfriend.
We drifted apart.

It was fun, some of the time,
while it lasted. You could say that,
I suppose, about most years,
about most lives.

Memorial

When I got home from Aunty Bob's funeral
I began to write a poem about her
but the man I was in love with phoned
and asked me out. I abandoned the poem
and never went back to it.

Miss Tucker. That was what they called her
in the shop. She was in charge
of haberdashery. Customers noticed
that she got on well with Mr Cartwright
of men's outfitting. A match, perhaps?

They had been married to each other
for years. He was Uncle Maurice,
a veteran of World War I, who never
mentioned it except to tell us, with a laugh,
that they all said 'Wipers' instead of 'Ypres'.

They laughed a lot, those two.
He recited comic monologues
as a party turn – 'Yon Lion's et Albert' –
and taught my sister to play pontoon.
Mummy wasn't happy about that.

They loved me and were always kind.
I loved them too. So, here's a small
memorial, three decades overdue.
The man who phoned? That didn't work out.
I wrote a dozen poems about him.

A Vow

I cannot promise never to be angry;
I cannot promise always to be kind.
You know what you are taking on, my darling –
It's only at the start that love is blind.

And yet I'm still the one you want to be with
And you're the one for me – of that I'm sure.
You are my closest friend, my favourite person,
The lover and the home I've waited for.

I cannot promise that I will deserve you
From this day on. I hope to pass that test.
I love you and I want to make you happy.
I promise I will do my very best.

To My Husband

If we were never going to die, I might
Not hug you quite as often or as tight,
Or say goodbye to you as carefully
If I were certain you'd come back to me.
Perhaps I wouldn't value every day,
Every act of kindness, every laugh
As much, if I knew you and I could stay
For ever as each other's other half.
We may not have too many years before
One disappears to the eternal yonder
And I can't hug or touch you any more.
Yes, of course that knowledge makes us fonder.
Would I want to change things, if I could,
And make us both immortal? Love, I would.

Calculations

I have been a non-smoker, now, for longer
                    than I was a smoker.

I have been a published poet almost as long
                    as I wasn't.

For more than half my adult years, I have earned a living
                    without having a job.

I have been fatherless for nearly two-thirds of my life.

In the run-up to our wedding I reflect that I will not be
        a married woman for half as long as I was single.

But, if we are both alive when I am 96, I will have had
            as many years with you as without you –

nearly a third of my life so far.

With luck, the fraction will grow, like evening sunlight
                 spreading across a field,

so the view at the end of the day is brighter and more
  beautiful

than I could have foreseen in the long, dark hours of
  the morning.

One Day

One day, my love, the good times will be over,
Never to return. And it could come
Quite suddenly – the news that either one
Of us is ill, unlikely to recover.
How will we deal with that – day after day
Of grief and sickness? Will we both be brave
And kind in everything we do and say
And, failing that, be able to forgive?
We'll have to do our best to stay afloat,
Despite our anger, tiredness and fear,
Trusting in our love, a sturdy boat
That's served us pretty well, year after year.
We'll hope it can survive the stormy weather
And bring us safely into port, together.

The Tree

We had to leave our home. We travelled here
With all our worldly goods – box after box
Of crockery and books, our furniture,
Our pictures, mirrors, lamps and rugs and clocks.
In its pot our precious Christmas tree,
A straggly adolescent, four years old,
Survived the journey, waited patiently
Till it was time to come in from the cold.
Now it's lit up in all its annual glory,
Hung with treasures taken out of store.
Every little trinket tells a story,
A memoir of the life we had before.
We got through the disruption and the pain.
The tree is telling us we're home again.

Here We Are

Here we are
in our small, chosen city,
happy to watch the ducks,
the narrowboats, the changing trees.

On the other side of the river
long goods trains trundle past.
Maersk, *China Shipping*,
China Shipping, *Maersk*.

Big world out there.
Ports, oceans, shopping districts.

We could be anywhere
but this is where we find ourselves,
happy to sit beside the river
and watch the trains go by.

Ely

for Mac Dowdy, historian

We thought our little city got its name
From eels. They have been caught and traded here
For centuries. The Isle of Eels became
The Isle of Ely. We liked that idea.
But there's a problem, since the word for eel,
Back when the early settlement was founded,
Was *anguilla* or *schlippen-fisch* or *aal*,
And no-one spoke of eels till 1300.
A newer theory, out of academe:
In ancient times this place was venerated
As holy, as a paradise. Its name,
As years went by, became abbreviated.
We like this even better: our new home
Is in a city called Elysium.

March 2013

The winter's going on and on.
The daffodils refuse to flower.
Like us, they're waiting for the sun.

They hug themselves inside the green
Through every icy gale and shower –
Through winter, going on and on.

St David's day has come and gone
And still they're waiting for the hour
When they can open in the sun.

One afternoon last week it shone
And briefly cheered us up before
It vanished. Winter's going on.

The sick and dying wonder when
The spring will come. Will they be here
When it arrives, with flowers and sun?

They hoped to see another one.
The skies aren't answering their prayer.
The winter's going on and on.
Like us, they're waiting for the sun.

Haiku: Willows

Willows white with frost:
like fireworks that whooshed, sparkled
and froze in the air.

Naga-Uta

Clearest of clear days:
frozen leaves under my feet,
frost on bare branches,
blue sky, smoke from the funnel
of a narrowboat,
and on the quiet river
great slicks of pale gold sunlight.

By the River

The day is so still
you can almost hear the heat.
You can almost hear
that royal blue dragonfly
landing on the old white boat.

Shakespeare at School

Forty boys on benches with their quills
Six days a week through almost all the year,
Long hours of Latin with relentless drills
And repetition, all enforced by fear.
I picture Shakespeare sitting near the back,
Indulging in a risky bit of fun
By exercising his prodigious knack
Of thinking up an idiotic pun,
And whispering his gem to other boys,
Some of whom could not suppress their mirth –
Behaviour that unfailingly annoys
Any teacher anywhere on earth.
The fun was over when the master spoke:
Will Shakespeare, come up here and share the joke.

The Marriage

Married at eighteen to a pregnant bride
Eight years your senior, did you think that you
Had spoiled your life before you'd even tried
To make your way and show what you could do?
Perhaps you loved each other and were glad
To tie the knot. Perhaps, each time you left
Your Anne, your little daughters and the lad
To set out on the road, you were bereft.
Perhaps you were relieved to get away.
Perhaps she was relieved to see you go.
Did you miss each other every day
And long for the return? We cannot know
The cost to you, your family, your wife.
We cannot wish you'd lived a different life.

On Sonnet 18

'So long as men can breathe and eyes can see' –
You don't assume we'll be around for ever.
You couldn't know that 'this gives life to thee'
Only until the sun goes supernova.
That knowledge doesn't prove your words untrue.
Neither time nor the advance of science
Has taken anything away from you,
Or faced down your magnificent defiance.
That couplet. Were you smiling as you wrote it?
Did you utter a triumphant 'Yes'?
Walking round the garden, did you quote it,
Sotto voce, savouring your success?
And did you always know, or sometimes doubt,
That passing centuries would bear you out?

The Worst Row

The worst row we two ever had concerned
The sonnets – Shakespeare's. I expressed the view
I'd held for years: that no-one could have turned
Those lines unless he was in love. 'Not true.
You'll find that all the academics say
You're wrong.' That pompous tone – the one that you
Use when you'll brook no argument. 'And they
Know better than mere poets?' 'Yes, they do.'
It happened in the car. I nearly stopped
And asked you to get out. Now I concede
That both of us were partly right. We dropped
The sulks before too long. But we're agreed
It *was* our worst dispute. The one we had
About a steak? That wasn't quite as bad.

My Father's Shakespeare

My father must have bought it secondhand,
Inscribed 'To R. S. Elwyn' – who was he?
Published 1890, leather-bound,
In 1961 passed on to me.
November 6th. How old was I? Sixteen.
Doing A level in English Lit.,
In love with Keats and getting very keen
On William Shakespeare. I was thrilled with it,
This gift, glad then, as now, to think
I had been chosen as the keeper of
My father's Shakespeare, where, in dark blue ink,
He wrote, 'To Wendy Mary Cope. With love.'
Love on a page, surviving death and time.
He didn't even have to make it rhyme.

At New Place

Not the one he planted but its 'scion',
According to the plaque, which I peruse
Close up, absorbed. I fail to keep an eye on
My feet till mulberry juice has ruined my shoes.
Pale grey lace-ups. Dark red fallen fruit.
And it's all Shakespeare's fault. If only he
Had chosen something different for this spot –
An oak, a sycamore, an apple tree.
I sit down on a nearby bench and think
Of Shakespeare with a sapling and a spade
And how this incident creates a link
Between us in the garden that he made.
I feel him smiling at me as he says
'Oh yes. The Muse works in mysterious ways.'

Young Love

School outing, 1960: *Romeo*
And Juliet. First time I'd seen a play
By Shakespeare on the stage. We had to go
By bus to the Old Vic. A matinée.
Don't know what I expected, probably
To find it rather boring. It was not.
Enchanted, I went back four times to see
The play again. I was in love. With what?
The characters (Mercutio!)? The actors –
Judi Dench and several dishy males?
The language? Maybe all of them were factors
Compelling me to boost the ticket sales
For Shakespeare plays as often as I could.
That teenage crush: I think it did me good.

If It Be Now

If it be now, 'tis not to come:
Hamlet, just before the fight
That sent him to eternal night.

It's always there: a quiet drum
Sounding when I have a fright:
If it be now, 'tis not to come.

Choking, breathless, falling – numb
With mortal fear, I hear it right
On cue and silently recite,
If it be now, 'tis not to come.

In Memory of Max Adrian 1903–1973

It's sad to think the actor never knew
About the teenage girl who saw him play
In *As You Like It* long ago and who
Can still recall his face and voice today:
His Jaques dignified, aloof and dry –
No bellowing, no sawing of the air,
Nothing that could offend the author's eye
Or ear, if you imagined he was there.
More than fifty years have passed since then
But when I read the text it's him I see,
And when I watch it on the stage again
Jaques doesn't stand a chance with me.
Max nailed the part and no-one else will do.
And that, it's possible to hope, he knew.

On Sonnet 22

My glass can't quite persuade me I am old –
In that respect my ageing eyes are kind –
But when I see a photograph, I'm told
The dismal truth: I've left my youth behind.
And when I try to get up from a chair
My knees remind me they are past their best.
The burden they have carried everywhere
Is heavier now. No wonder they protest.
Arthritic fingers, problematic neck,
Sometimes causing mild to moderate pain,
Could well persuade me I'm an ancient wreck
But here's what helps me to feel young again:
My love, who fell for me so long ago,
Still loves me just as much, and tells me so.

A Wreath for George Herbert

Dear George, although I do not share your faith,
A faith expressed in poems I revere,
Revere and love, I offer you this wreath,
A wreath of words, like yours, although I fear,
I fear it won't be worthy of the man,
The awe-inspiring man who loved to play,
To play with words, to make them rhyme and scan,
Scan and rhyme and at the same time say,
Say something true: the truth about your fear,
Your fear, your anger and your love. A wreath,
A humble wreath for someone I revere,
Revere and love, though I can't share your faith.

A Poem about Jesus

When I find myself feeling sorry for the wrong people –
disgraced politicians, vilified bankers,
the victims of paedophile witch-hunts –
I remember that Jesus was the friend of sinners
and he would have felt sorry for them too.

I love him for that. And I love him
for being on the side of the wusses,
telling us the meek will inherit the earth.

I don't know if he was the son of God.
I don't know if he rose from the grave.
If he is a fiction,
the genius who created him
deserves all the love and the praise we can give.

Little Donkey

The children's favourite. We had
to sing it in the Christmas concert
every year, plodding along
with me at the piano, and a child
going clip-clop with coconut shells
or woodblock: a coveted job.

It wasn't my favourite.
After I left teaching
I forgot about it
for more than ten years

until one day, near Christmas,
in a busy high street
a Salvation Army band
began to play it. I stood still

with tears in my eyes.
Little Donkey. All those children
who loved it so much.
All those hands in the air
begging to be chosen
to make the sound of his hooves.

Lantern Carol

At the winter solstice,
Midnight of the year,
A lantern in a stable
Shows us He is here.

Shining through the ages,
Lighting up the place
Where we see the baby,
His little hands, his face,

A lantern in a stable
Centuries ago
Conquers time and darkness
With its gentle glow,

Calls us with the shepherds
And the eastern kings,
Offers us the Christ child
And the love He brings.

In the golden lamplight,
See him there asleep.
Ours if we will have Him.
Ours to love and keep.

Christmas Cards

Cards to the very old
go out like doves
who will bring back news
of one kind or another.

It may be a sign of life –
a few sentences
in a shaky hand,
I hope that you are well.

It may be a letter
from a friend or relative
who found my address on the back:
I am very sorry to tell you . . .

This year two cards,
both to widowers,
came winging back with labels:
Addressee gone away.

I open my Christmas list,
find their names
and type *d.2016.*
I could remove them

but that would leave
no trace of them
and I am not quite ready
for them to disappear.

In Memory of Dennis O'Driscoll

After I heard that you had died
I went and found your Christmas card –
People round a tree.
Inside, a message written days
Before, and all in upper case,
Of course, for L. and me.

You mention 'Our reunion
In Dublin'. That took place in June –
A reading on a date
When all of Ireland had to see
A football match. Our poetry
Could not compete with that.

It didn't matter much to me.
I'd flown across the Irish Sea
Because you asked me to,
Though not imagining, dear friend,
That you had nearly reached the end
Until I looked at you –

So very thin, so very pale.
How could you not be gravely ill?
You said you were OK –
Some minor problem, sorted now.
Whatever else you feared or knew
You were not going to say.

No more envelopes from you,
Bold capitals announcing who
Had written us a letter.
Those letters were so generous
With warmth, intelligence and praise,
They made us both feel better.

I hope you knew how much it meant –
Your interest, your encouragement.
I hope I made it clear
That you were high up on my list
Of favourite people. You'll be missed
As long as I am here.

In Memory of a Psychoanalyst

Arthur S. Couch 1924–2015

1 *The Kleinians*

Your funeral. And on the day
The Kleinians were crying.
Your vilified opponents. They
Turned up for you on that sad day
And wept. I wonder what you'd say –
Some quip about the perks of dying?
I wish you knew that on the day
The Kleinians were crying.

2 Dreams

I had a dream about Nanna.
I was walking in her funeral procession
and she was walking beside me,
alive and well.

You talked about ambivalence:
I wanted her back
but I was tired
of worrying about her.

I had a dream about you,
a dream I won't be telling you,
now you're gone, now
I can only tell the page.

You came to see us, you
and a friend, a woman analyst.
We sat and talked. It was
a pleasant occasion.

When you left, you walked
a little way, then turned to wave.
That image of you, well and happy,
has brought you back

the way you were before
your wife died, before
the years of loneliness,
before you were ill.

It seems (as you would say)
it seems I have a wish
to see you restored to health
and with a companion,

a wish for you to visit me
and meet my husband,
to stay a little while
and then go cheerfully away.

I miss you sometimes
but I'm not felled by grief.
It seems that's how it should be.
It seems you did a good job.

A Little Tribute to John Cage

'Wherever we are, what we hear is mostly
noise. When we ignore it, it disturbs us.
When we listen to it, we find it fascinating.'
– John Cage

My computer humming
while triangles dance on the screen.

A blackbird singing,
perched on the garden gate.

The soft scratch of my pencil
as I write these words.

A trio for computer,
blackbird and pencil.

One continuous sound, one random,
one controlled by me.

The pencil's part is almost over.
When it stops

A Statue

Here is a statue of a man who died
Nearly thirty years ago. He stands
On one leg, in a dancing pose, beside
The sea, near children playing on the sands.
People with cameras form a little queue.
In turn the men adopt the dancing pose.
I'm touched to see what all the women do:
They hug the statue's arm and nestle close.
Is there another statue anywhere
That people treat like this? Can't think of one.
The man wears specs, has lost most of his hair,
Inspires affection that goes on and on.
The town? The man? Both answers are the same:
Morecambe. Eric Morecambe is the name.

Cento

for Fleur Adcock

Art's whatever you choose to frame.
It looks easy enough. Let's try it.

I got a Gold Star for the Pilgrim Fathers
but I don't suppose that counts, does it?

In the dream I was kissing John Prescott.
No-one ever notices his ears.

All the worse things come stalking in
and I am still a day off 70.

Somehow we manage to like our friends,
but now that I am in love with a place

one day is enough to remember.
It makes me laugh. In fact, it makes me sing.

Where's a Pied Piper
When You Need One?

Headline in the *Daily Telegraph*, 25 May 2012

In 'The Pied Piper of Hamelin' by Robert Browning
Thousands of rats are led to the river and to death
    by drowning.
A good story but not a true one: no-one sensible
    believes a word of it.
None the less, tourists flock to Hamelin because they
    have heard of it.
Tourists spend money and make a place richer,
But, sad to recount, that is not the whole pitcher.
Visitors leave litter, some of it edible, and that's
Why Hamelin has a problem, and the problem is
    RATS.
When they've finished their dinner they go back
    underground
And gnaw through any cables that are lying around.
The traffic lights stop working and so does the
    fountain.
Council workmen have repaired them so many times
    they have stopped countin',
Which brings me at last to the burden of my song:
Next time someone quotes Auden saying 'Poetry
    makes nothing happen', you can tell them he was
    wrong.

On a Photograph of the Archbishop
of Canterbury

You see an archbishop out jogging in shorts.
You know it's unfair to have negative thoughts.

There's no reason at all why he shouldn't keep fit.
It's commendable. You can't help sneering a bit

And thinking of Becket and Cranmer and Laud
And numerous others, who may have been flawed,

But of whom, I believe it is safe to say, none
Ever took off his trousers and went for a run.

Of course, things are tough for archbishops today –
Nasty photographers snapping away.

It's nasty of me to write this. I confess it.
I don't think I'm sorry enough to suppress it.

Men Talking

Anecdotes and jokes,
On and on and on.
If you're with several blokes,
It's anecdotes and jokes.

If you were to die
Of boredom, there and then,
They'd notice, by and by,
If you were to die.

But it could take a while.
They're having so much fun.
You neither speak nor smile.
It could take a while.

At 70

Of fitness and vitality I am not the epitome.
I sometimes think there's something wrong with nearly
   every bit o' me.
My teeth are wearing out. I cannot give them
   a sabbatical,
And finding shoes that will not hurt my feet is
   problematical.
My hearing isn't what it was. I fear that's undeniable.
My memory? It may be just a fraction less reliable.
I cannot read a word unless my glasses are available.
The view that I am somewhat overweight is
   unassailable.

That's been a lifelong struggle. I'm not ready to
   surrender yet.
I'm very careful what I eat. I dream that I'll be slender
   yet.
I might stay healthy longer if I were a vegetarian,
But I'm not doing badly for a septuagenarian.

My blood tests came back fine when they were sent off
   for analysis.
I'm lucky not to be on chemo or to need dialysis.
My hips and knees are bearing up. They do not want
   replacing yet
And cardiac anxieties are something I'm not facing yet.

It might be better for my health if I were less
dogmatical
And didn't freak out when a news report is
ungrammatical
Or when a word is mispronounced. If someone says
'mischievious',
I want to shake them and explain it doesn't rhyme
with devious.

Please don't call me sprightly, as I may react
aggressively
And use my sprightly tongue to speak a little too
expressively.
Perhaps I am intolerant, a tad authoritarian,
But I'm not doing badly for a septuagenarian.

I do some boring exercises to improve mobility.
I don't know if there's anything that helps postpone
senility.
I do a crossword every day. I play with forms poetical
With one as tough as this I sometimes get a bit
frenetical.
I borrowed it from Gilbert's lines about the 'Major-
Gineral',
Where even Gilbert had to cheat to make it rhyme
with mineral,
Since nothing rhymes with General. The problem was
intractable
But no-one minds because his song's so singable and
actable.

Gilbert was a genius who always got the metre right.
It is my modest hope that I have counted up these feet
  aright.
Where prosody's concerned, I've never been a
  libertarian
And I'm not changing now that I'm a septuagenarian.

Health Advice

'People who read books enjoy a significant
"survival advantage" over those who do not.'
– report in *The Times*, 5 August 2016, on a survey
published in *Social Science and Medicine*

If you want to stay alive,
Sit and read a book.
It will help you to survive.
If you want to stay alive,
Eat broccoli and you may thrive
But here's the good news – look:
If you want to stay alive,
Sit and read a book.

New Year

The year has died. Another year is born
And people party, set the sky ablaze.
Puzzled by their happiness, I mourn
The passing of so many precious days.
Enjoyed or squandered, they won't come again.
Out there the world is celebrating. Why?
The solemn midnight tolling of Big Ben
Tells us we're nearer to the day we'll die.
They know that too. Perhaps it's why they drink
And congregate in crowds to cheer and sing.
Is it denial? Do they really think
Time moving on is such a joyful thing?
I used to make an effort to be glad.
Not now. I stay home feeling old and sad.

Tallis's Canon

One of the things I'd like to do again
before I die is sing Tallis's Canon
in canon with other voices, using the words
written by the saintly Thomas Ken
for the use of the scholars of Winchester College:
Glory to thee my God this night
For all the blessings of the light.

It's years since I sang that hymn,
except to myself, or taught a child
to play it on the recorder.
I want to have it at my funeral,
not sung in canon – that would be
too complicated, and, anyway,
I wouldn't be there to join in the fun.

What a pity. I'd like everyone to imagine
how much I would have enjoyed
organising a churchful of people
into four parts, bringing them in
at the right moment, and singing my heart out:
Keep me, O keep me, King of kings,
Beneath thine own almighty wings.

Que Sera

The song was 'Que Sera, Sera'.
We sang and sang it in the car
Till Daddy called a halt.

Fatalistic and carefree –
That wasn't him. It isn't me –
Worriers to a fault,

Always keen to organise
The future, though the enterprise
Is sculpting water.

It goes on flowing anyhow.
Daddy has no future now
And mine is shorter.

As my last years cascade away
Moving faster every day,
The song comes back to me,

Saying you can't change what's coming,
Just let go and keep on humming
What will be, will be.

Every

Every ditch or stream or river the train crosses.
Every ploughed field, every row of trees.
Every square church tower in the distance.
Every minute of sunshine, every shadow.
Every wisp of cloud in the wide, blue, East
    Anglian sky.
Every day. Every day that's left.